Before the Sun

Before the Sun

Poems by

Peter Schireson

Cover design by Shay Culligan
Cover image by Nicolas Moscarda
Author's photo by Peter Schireson

ISBN: 978-1-63980-302-6

Kelsay Books
502 South 1040 East, A-119
American Fork, Utah 84003
Kelsaybooks.com

Acknowledgments

The following poems have appeared previously, sometimes in different versions or with different titles:

Third Wednesday: "In Which I Consider My Ancestors"

Triggerfish Critical Review: "Hosanna," "In the Small Café,"
  "How the Day Begins"

Contents

My grandfather sits atop a large white horse, squinting into the light. On the back of the photo: "1931, Smoketree Ranch." He has moved the family from New York City to Palm Springs in the wake of the stock market crash and the collapse of his health. They remain in Palm Springs for two years, then move to Los Angeles. Ninety years later, in the midst of a pandemic, my wife and I move from New York City to Palm Springs, giving birth to these poems.

Pandemic Diary Excerpts

Togetherness and banishment,
wife and I smoldering on the living room couch,
our tiny continent.

I open the amazon packages.
She reminds me to wash my hands.
I escape into her beauty.

From the window, I watch my neighbor
kiss his dog on the mouth.
Life through a telescope.

Mornings are inexhaustible.
What to talk about?
Our poop vocabulary is expanding;
two current favorites:
Night Train to Memphis,
Children of a Lesser God.
Mornings are exhausting.

Sitting in the back yard,
a lone bird floats across my peripheral vision,
a blurred half-silhouette, like a mystic sign.
Time of lost time.

Every day I walk through the neighborhood
past faceless windows and overgrown lawns.
I am hungry from morning to night.
Is it this easy to undo the world?

I am a swamp of murky thoughts.
I try not to dwell, but fear creeps into me,
my body charged with mortality.
Last night, dreams filled with trees,
the trees full of crows.

The house draws into itself.
I am mesmerized by my metabolism.
Life through a microscope.

We need to move.

Dogged

Our afternoon hike behind us, Dog and I turn
and head for home.
Twilight spills over the hills, ridgeline trees
  in shaggy outline.
Bright yellow petals blanket the ground—
Palo Verdes blown loose by the freewheeling wind.

We left an imprisoned city that heaved with rage,
for the hum of leaves and an unlocked door.
Walking this way with Dog every day,
the city fades slowly away,
finding its place in memory, replaced by this new place.

Almost there, from a short block off,
I watch a UPS truck pull away from our house,
box on the sidewalk next to our gate.
From the size of that box,
it must be the dog bed we bought for you, Dog.
Tilting his head, Dog looks up at the sound of his name,

then back toward our house, where a small black sedan
skids to a stop; a young man jumps out, grabs the box,
and speeds off.
It's the second theft in as many months,
the first, my bike from the yard the day we moved in.

I sit on a bench, letting the afternoon's drama dim.
A hush flows into our yard. The dark comes down
and night settles in, quiet except for the low hum
of cars passing beyond our gate.
Dog sleeps on the grass at my feet, twitches, turns.

Road Signs

for John Adler

My late seventies,
a tricky stretch of downhill road,
my brakes creak and I'm low on gas,
infirmity lurks,

but there's an odd comfort in the decline—
watching the sun slump behind the high hills,
the dark spreading across the sand,
slivers of last light flashing on the fronds—

and for a moment, it's as if, before slipping into night,
time is facing backwards,
a bemused glance over its shoulder at the fading day.

Corner Café

Now I must decide:
the Pecan, smelling of acacia honey,
the comfort of the Peach Crumble,
the Pumpkin achingly golden,
or the magnetic Oreo crust on the Chocolate Cream.

Would you like extra whipped cream with that?
The waitress, Dolores, leans forward,
grins a goofy grin.
Her nylon dress rustles like summer snow.

Having finished my Chocolate Cream,
I walk out into the great impartial calm.
Her words continue to swarm in my ears.

I mold my lips into a kiss,
raise my hands to my face, and look up,
the clouds huge in the sky,
my eyes huge in the clouds.

Xerophilia

I remember sitting next to uncle S at a family brunch,
my high school "Hamlet" text open on my lap.
Uncle S, who's been dozing, opens one eye
and glances down at the book.
I recite the line, *To be, or not to be,* whereupon
Uncle S shuts his open eye and continues,
that is the question . . .
and proceeds to recite the entire soliloquy.

Wandering through this cactus garden,
I think about the men of my father's generation.
Cacti define the landscape in the desert—
dignified, mysterious, a little alien, forbidding.
They are frugal, flowering only occasionally.
I stop to admire a Kingcup specimen
in full annual claret-red bloom.
My hand is drawn to a blossom.
I rub my palm where I am pierced.

Hunting

I stared at the monitor above my father's bed
watching the green line bending stubbornly down
until it was a snake.
Holding my father's hand,
I could feel his bright warmth leaking out.

When we got home from the hospital,
mother tried to comfort us all.
She asked me if there was anything of my father's
        I wanted.
I opened his closet and touched the alpaca sweater
I once lusted after.
It was small in my adult hands, color faded
like an old Polaroid.

Just once, on a trip to the desert,
I went quail hunting with him,
and, after winging one, I found it flapping in the grass.
It's done for, he said.
Just take its head in your fingers and twist it quick.
I couldn't do it.
He smiled. *It's okay.*
He, of course, could.

In the Sweet Gold

Sometimes I imagine
accompanying the dying in their dying,
walking with them toward a bridge
in the sweet gold of a late afternoon.

At 77, an abridged version of myself,
I approach slowly, rapt in the singularity of the moment,
the bridge suspended above the desert in space,
hanging on nothing.

The curve of time eases me on,
across the bridge and into night,
ushering me into emptiness.
Where my thoughts once were,
a formless mist.
A life burned down,
I leave little trace.
The world no longer needs me,
if it ever did.

Before the Sun

Ahead of the sluggish heat,
the air lush with citrus bloom,
a dry wind rushes over the hills,
landscape's edges—cactus, boulder, palm—
almost in focus.

A small host of finches gossip in the grass.
I move closer, a grey shape intruding
on their grey morning.
In their bird-frame, I am neither pattern nor detail,
I am nobody, a current of shadow,
a blur,
like a leaf bown against a fence.

First drops of light spill onto the earth.
The finches fly off.
I kneel down, dig my fingers into the sand,
and peer into the sublime indifference of the warming day.

In the desert just before the sun appears,
morning is a kind of heaven,
in which I am free to be myself,
or no one.

Overheated

In summer, the desert heat carries a sweet, smoky smell,
as if of burning flesh, as if I could myself combust.[1]
I respond with defiance,[2]
but my defiance is misplaced,
for the heat is inescapable,[3]

---

[1] The term "spontaneous human combustion" was first proposed in a journal article in *Philosophical Transactions of the Royal Society* in 1746, written by Paul Rolli, a Fellow of the Royal Society, concerning the death of Countess Cornelia Zangheri Bandi. Rolli writes,

"The Countess Cornelia Bandi, in the 62d *[sic]* . . . Year of her Age, was all Day as well as she used to be; but at Night was observed, when at Supper, dull and heavy . . . In the Morning, the Maid . . . went into the Bed-chamber, and called her; but not being answer'd, doubting of some ill Accident, open'd the Window, and saw the Corpse of her Mistress in this deplorable Condition. Four Feet Distance from the Bed there was a Heap of Ashes, two Legs untouched, from the Foot to the Knee, with their Stockings on; between them was the Lady's head; whose Brains, Half of the Backpart of the Scull, and the whole Chin, were burnt to Ashes; amongst which were found three Fingers blacken'd. All the rest was Ashes, which had this particular Quality, that they left in the Hand, when taken up, a greasy and stinking Moisture . . . "

Furniture and linen in the room were left untouched by the conflagration.

[2] Like Humphrey Bogart in the 1943 film, "Sahara." Bogart plays American tank commander Joe Gunn, his tank and crew in retreat across the Sahara after the fall of Tobruk. They find their way to a desert well, whereupon a German battalion arrives. The heat is oppressive and the well runs dry, but Gunn tricks the parched Germans into thinking otherwise, and a battle of wills begins between Gunn and the German commander, Major von Falken. The Germans mount attacks, but Gunn holds them off. In this analogy, I am Joe Gunn and the heat is Major von Falken.

[3] A monk asked Zen master Tung-shan (807–869), "When cold or heat comes, how can I escape it?" Tung-shan replied, "Why don't you go to a place where there is no cold or heat?" "What's it like in a place where there is neither cold nor heat?" asked the monk. Tung-shan said,"When it's cold, you are exceedingly cold; when it is hot, you are exceedingly hot."

and so I've learned to respect the heat's intransigence,
albeit grudgingly,[4]
and when at last, the sun retreats behind the hills,
and the burning heat departs,
I wonder, where has it gone?[5]

---

[4] In the 1995 film, "Heat," Robert de Niro and Al Pacino met on-screen for the first time. Pacino plays a cop, Vincent Hanna, in pursuit of de Niro's character, Neil McCauley, a career thief. In one famous scene, Hanna and McCauley have a quiet conversation over coffee in a small diner. Each knows the other's role. Even as the scene ends with both acknowledging one is almost certain to kill the other next time they meet, it's clear that Hanna respects McCauley's professionalism. In this scene, I am Hanna, the heat is McCauley.

[5] In 1667, Johann Joachim Becher proposed the existence of phlogiston, an element released from objects during combustion. According to the theory, objects dephlogisticate when they burn, stored phlogiston is released into the air, and absorbed by plants.

Church

Returning from our every evening walk,
Dog pees on the usual rocks.
Also, tonight, on my right shoe.
In the slow fatigue of dusk,
a band of haze floats over the neighborhood,
the air perfumed with mesquite.
A finch hops into frame,
taciturn,
hops off.
I release Dog from his leash.
Let loose, he leaps out of himself
and races up and down the block,
a scruffy masterpiece of total exertion.
Palms sway in the breeze like a gospel choir.

Insomnia

Middle of another night,
my mind colonized by the evening's headlines.
It seems like the world is losing all its tenderness.

I try to fall asleep by counting my breath.
I imagine myself a wakeful dream, dreaming itself.
I review the day—a white Corvette convertible
ablaze with sunlight, smoke from barbecues
drifting over the neighborhood,
ghost vapors rising out of the sidewalk,
a man at a bus stop tearing up pieces of paper.

Lying perfectly still, suspended
between the soft witchery of words
and the rough skin of the world,
I doze on and off.

Thirst

First June rain in the desert in more than forty years.
The scorched hills open their bare arms,
and the earth is cloaked in the scent of wet, settled dust.
Tilting my head to the liquid sky,
I breathe in the musky petrichor, feeling myself rise
as if I am floating high above the scrub,
gazing across the dunes bright with silence and bone, until,
quick as it came, the rain retires,
driven off by a dry wind. In its wake,
the bare sensation of being alive,
smell of sand and chaparral, hints of eucalyptus,
the small laughter of birds.

Ancestors

How they wandered in the desert,
how they bowed their heads to pray,
how they bowed their heads to blend in,
how, robbed of their rings, they sang
and drummed upon their own skin,
until their skin was taken away,

how they lived in shelters of bark,
lived in buildings with chickens and knife fights,
endorsed heaven and enclosed themselves with a wire*,
and made with the wire a province of inside,
wheels inside wheels, water in water,
fish inside men, lakes inside women,

how they pulled the wire taut around all they cherished,
all in accord with the scalding judgment of their god,
babies and medicines, canes and keys,
the laws and their songs, all saved
by the strength of the wire.

---

* The wire in this poem refers to an *eruv*, an urban area enclosed by a wire boundary which symbolically extends the private domain of Jewish households into public areas, permitting activities within it that are normally forbidden in public on the Sabbath.

Scenes of My Mother

Palm Springs, 1958, under a hammered copper sun:
poolside at the motel, my mother wears a one-piece
    bathing suit, a wide-brimmed hat.
I hand her her iced tea. She applauds playfully.
Thank you, dear.

Hollywood, 2010, a snapshot taped to her kitchen wall
of two young Polish girls, eight or nine years old.
Along the edge she's scrawled a single word in pencil:
"Sobibor."
The Germans gassed them, she says.
It could have been me, but my parents fled.
If theirs had fled and they'd survived . . .
Her voice falters. *I had better luck.*

Hollywood, near the end,
a hospital bed in her living room,
she wakes from her morphine-assisted sleep.
Please remind me, dear . . . is what I have fatal?
Yes, I say, *it is.*
That is helpful to know. Thank you, dear.

Waiting to See the Neurologist

I'm waiting to see the neurologist.
That awakening lurch at the onset of sleep
has become a nightlong jitterbug,
and my once soothing snore has swollen to a roar
that lifts me out of our marital bed
and onto the guest room couch.
House keys and loose change incarcerated
      in a jacket pocket
have made another getaway, re-captured only by luck,
cowering under a French fry bag behind the front seat
      of the car.
Names I recently learned—the fishing guide's
and the Italian waiter's—are discernible
only in vague outline through a haze of random syllables.
And the Chinese characters I've been wooing for years
are as fickle as seventh grade girlfriends.
I'm ignoring them all,
until I have seen the neurologist.

Day before Surgery

The afternoon news is angry, tribal—
I switch it off.
Dog looks up from his bed and we walk together
into the silence of the yard—
the sun, perched on the rim of the western hills,
bathes the valley in candied light.

I sit on a bench my father and I made,
longing for his company:
too easy to remember his death,
groping to remember his life.
An image bobs in my mind like foam on a wave—
my mother's shadow on the wall outside his hospital room door,
pacing, pacing.

It's December, the flowers lining the yard fading.
Dog races around in his manic, plotless ballet,
jumping onto my lap, licking my chin.
Long shadows crawl across the grass
in the adamant dusk.

.

Hosanna

The door of the corner convenience store opens
into the company of everything.
I enter astride my senses,
bathed in the whispers of low-fat yoghurt,
my childhood echoes among the foiled mints,
the sounds come to my ears,
my ears go to the sounds.
Perfume rises from the spicy wings,
fluorescence spills over me,
over the Flaming Hot Nacho Tortilla Chips,
over the gummy bears, squirming in their lucite bins
like prehistoric creatures.
My eyes roam over the aisles of toilet paper
          and paper towels,
as outside across the parking lot, a persimmon sun rises
behind the smog, as if a great jewel forming in heaven.

In Which I Consider the Weather

A New York friend says
we have no real seasons in the Coachella Valley.

Untrue.

Come fall, the death of summer, and we feel like feathers.
Birds prance like runway models on the telephone wires,
leaves toss in the twilight wind.

Winter keeps us cool—
the last of the fall leaves look up from under the trees
as if on the verge of speech.

With Spring, freckles of peppery warmth,
a wonderment in the blood,
nerves purr, and the abyss holds off.

Then Summer—early mornings, the air still benign, bright,
even clarifying.
But by eleven, images begin to dissolve—
a dog crosses the street, a crow lands on the fence—
a succession of blurry moments,
mopped up, one by one, by the burgeoning heat.

Across the street, two doves park in a palm
above a pink couple from Minnesota
on their third poolside margarita,
committing slow suicide by sunburn.

To walk outside is to wobble between reverence, collapse,
and a kind of puzzlement: Can it really be this hot?
Why, for the love of God, are we living here?

We try not to think about it.
We try to regroup—
we swim, we air-condition,
we cocktail, we reconstitute,
but the vast, untractable heat has pinned us down,
songbirds shuttered, sidewalks barren, car-less streets.
A hummingbird hovers over the bougainvillea
as if to paraphrase the simmering silence.

At eleven, the shiny woman on Channel Seven proclaims,
Tomorrow's expected high: One hundred-twelve,
and the expectation of blistering heat forms
into a noose around the neck of another day.

Vestigial

First you feel it raw
on your face, sharp,
and wherever you are thereafter,
you never feel heat again
without recalling
that depth of summer desert heat,
rising in waves,
suffusing the air,
sucking it in,
mouthfuls of it,
intransigent,
choking.
It never leaves you . . .
heartless, erotic heat.

What We Desire Rules Over Us

The sun sets across the hills,
night, bright butterfly, unfolds its wings.
Streetlights crackle along the sidewalk,
the flowering trees grow talkative with hummingbirds,
the breeze a soft, singing sound,
like sand blowing off the crest of a dune.

As the scent of dry grass settles like snow
over the gleaming sanctuaries of luxury goods,
groups of teen girls strut the main drag,
dressed to drive their mothers mad.
Young men stroll hand in hand,
old men sip coffee at outdoor tables,
amused, but unbewitched.
Figures disappear into doorways
like snakes into cracks in the rocks.

Insomnia

Night after night, the past snakes through my mind
like a B movie, replete with complexity, deception,
betrayal, loyalty, pride,
but without a satisfactory conclusion.
Will it ever finish with me?
Last night, it showed up as I tried to sleep,
stood by my bed, frowned, and led me on a walk
through my old neighborhood.

The neighborhood, once lovely,
was now a place of un-mowed lawns and dirt sidewalks.
A volatile dog paced the street.
We had to step around the trash.

And even though I knew my father had died, there he was,
standing in front of my childhood house;
it was crumbling now like an old foam mattress.
When I asked him what he'd been doing,
he frowned and said he'd been observing me
from the other world,
waiting for me as I circled the drain,

which got me up and out of bed,
to spend the rest of the night prowling
through my medical charts online
in a fog of shadowy fears, fears of things I cannot name
and have no idea how to fix.
I shambled around the house like a penguin 'til dawn,
started the coffee, and emailed Dr. V for an appointment,
hoping for the dullness of a routine exam.

I Cry Aloud, But There Is No Judgement

The heat takes my hand.
I look into its eyes,
the surrounding expanse delicate and immense.
It holds my stare.

As if under a spell,
my thoughts like smears of paint,
I feel a need to explain myself,
to speak out loud to the heat
about who I am, who I've been.
I hear myself sing a line from "I'm a Fool to Want You"—
Time and again, I went away.

The lyric reaches out like a drowning man's hand
grasping for a rope.
I pause for the heat's reply.

Article of Faith

Up at dawn, I walk with Dog through the neighborhood,
desert stretching away to the east, sky filling up with blue.
Doves murmur in the mesquite.

My mind swirls in search of words
adequate to just this,
a search for the inexpressible within the expressible.

I close my eyes and begin to make my way
along the slippery surface of language.
Words well up in search of a poem:

It's like a first brief touch between two people . . .
It's as if time has coiled around itself . . .
It's like a hungry circling hawk . . .
It's like dissolving . . .

About the Author

Peter Schireson grew up in California, earned a BA from UC Berkeley, an M.Ed. at University of Victoria, and an Ed.D. from Harvard University. After retiring from a career, first in education and later in business, he returned to school to earn an MFA from The Program for Writers at Warren Wilson College. In addition to poems in journals, he has published three chapbooks—*The Welter of Me and You, The Salt,* and *What Worlds and Moons*—and two full length collections of poems—*Sword of Glass* (Broadstone Books) and *How We Met* (Kelsay Books). He is also an ordained Zen Buddhist priest, having trained in both the US and Japan. He is married to the psychologist and Zen teacher, Grace Jill Schireson, with whom he co-edited *Zen Bridge: The Zen Teachings of Keido Fukushima.* Peter and Jill divide their time between Palm Springs and Solana Beach, California.

www.ingramcontent.com/pod-product-compliance
Lightning Source LLC
Chambersburg PA
CBHW030815090426
42737CB00010B/1287